To Chuck and Jan, our favorite captain and admiral

4880 Lower Valley Road • Atglen, PA 19310

Other Schiffer Books by the Authors:
Double-Talk: Word Sense and Nonsense, 978-0-7643-3962-2, $14.99
Busy Bodies: Play Like the Animals, 978-0-7643-3832-8, $14.99
A to Z: Pick What You'll Be, 978-0-7643-3701-7, $14.99

Other Schiffer Books on Related Subjects:
ABCs of Boating Terms, 978-0-7643-3982-0, $6.99
U.S. Life Saving Coloring Book, 978-0-7643-3483-2, $6.99

ISBN: 978-0-7643-4184-7
Printed in China

Published by Schiffer Publishing, Ltd.
4880 Lower Valley Road
Atglen, PA 19310
Phone: (610) 593-1777; Fax: (610) 593-2002
E-mail: Info@schifferbooks.com

For the largest selection of fine reference books on this and related subjects, please visit our website at **www.schifferbooks.com.**
You may also write for a free catalog.

This book may be purchased from the publisher.
Please try your bookstore first.

We are always looking for people to write books on new and related subjects. If you have an idea for a book, please contact us at
proposals@schifferbooks.com

Schiffer Books are available at special discounts for bulk purchases for sales promotions or premiums. Special editions, including personalized covers, corporate imprints, and excerpts can be created in large quantities for special needs. For more information contact the publisher.

In Europe, Schiffer books are distributed by
Bushwood Books
6 Marksbury Ave.
Kew Gardens
Surrey TW9 4JF England
Phone: 44 (0) 20 8392 8585; Fax: 44 (0) 20 8392 9876
E-mail: info@bushwoodbooks.co.uk
Website: www.bushwoodbooks.co.uk

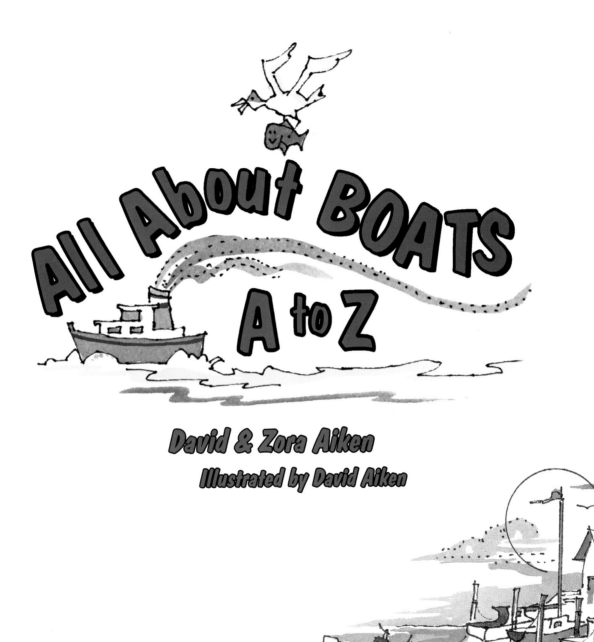

All About BOATS
A to Z

David & Zora Aiken

Illustrated by David Aiken

The **anchor** drops down,
Boat stops on the spot.
Be sure it's tied on,
Or anchored, you're *not!*

a A

B b

A ship's **bell** works well.
It sends out its sound
To say the boat's there
When fog is all 'round.

The **compass** marks North,
And East, South, and West.
It shows where to aim
To steer the boat best.

D d

The **dinghy's** a small boat
For all kinds of fun.
We row it or sail it
All day in the sun.

The **ensign's** a boat flag
To fly when we ride.
It's made just for boats—
We show it with pride.

F f

A **fender** protects
The side of the hull,
So bumps on the dock
Won't make the hull dull.

The **galley's** a kitchen.
Here, cook stows the food.
A bunch of good snacks,
Gives crew a good mood.

H h

A **horn** is most handy
When you need to call
A boat or bridgetender.
Its *honk* reaches all.

Watch **instruments** closely—
The boat stays on track.
They show course and speed
And how to get back.

i l

J j

With a **jib** sail set forward
The boat can keep pace.
A big jib or small one
Can help win the race.

Most boats have a **keel**—
It's part of design.
A sailboat's deep keel
Helps hold a straight line.

The right word is **line**,
For rope used on board.
OK to say "dockline,"
But never "dock cord."

The **motor** has power
To make the boat go.
It pushes and turns,
It even can tow.

m M

N n

Sometimes a big **needle**
Can fix a bad tear.
On sail or on canvas,
Repair anywhere.

Two **oars** for the dinghy
Can be a "plan B."
If outboard konks out,
You're not stuck at sea.

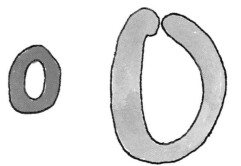

P p

Remember these letters:
"**P-F-D**," you'll say,
To ask for a life vest
To wear on boat days.

The **quarterberth** (or bunk)
Is not often slept in.
It's just right to stow
The crew's duffle bags in.

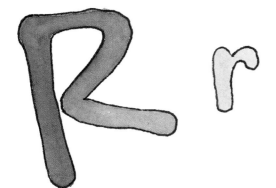

The **radar** can find things
In fog or at night.
You "see" them on screen
Instead of by sight.

"Sou'wester"—a good hat
To wear on rain days.
Its big yellow brim
Sends rain drops away.

The **transom's** the place where
The boat's name should be.
The back of the boat
Is easy to see.

Who wears **uniforms**?
The Coast Guard's young men.
They inspect for safety
On boats now and then.

V v

A **vent** catches air,
And brings it inside.
The boat will stay fresh
And cool for your ride.

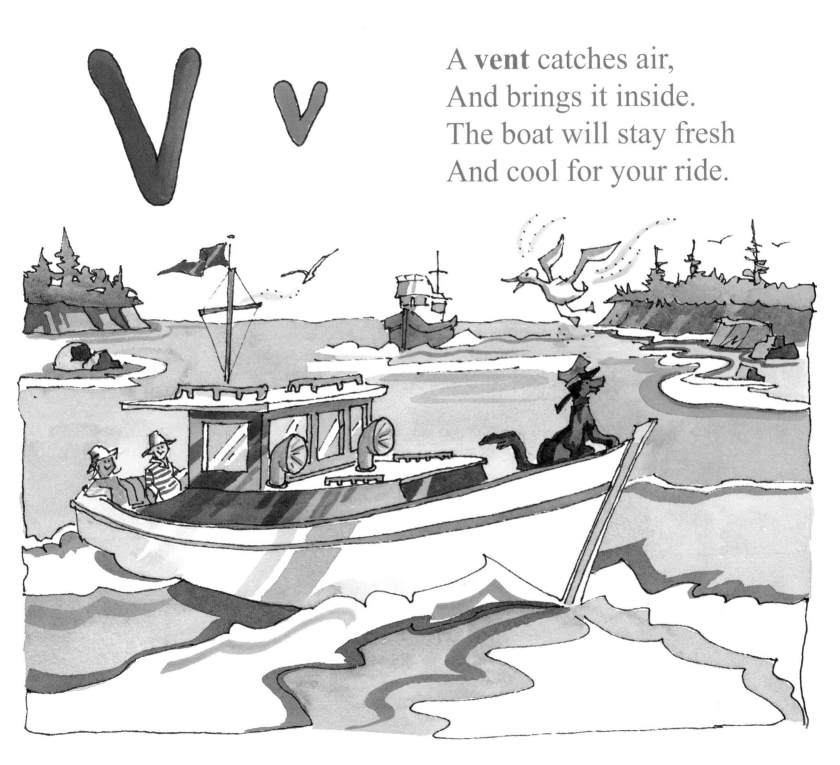

The steering **wheel** turns
To *port* or to *starboard*.
It keeps you on course
From harbor to harbor.

For X think **eXtinguisher**:
It fights fire, we hear.
We don't want a fire, but
Boats need safety gear.

A **yawl** is a sailboat
With sails on two masts.
A main and a mizzen
Will help it go fast.

A sailboat **"zigzags"**
To one side, then back.
(The sailors on board
Call each move a tack.)

A to Z boating
Does not mean you're done.
The more that you learn,
The more you'll have fun.